Praise for

OUR VALUED CUSTOMERS

"Everything you've heard a comic geek say in a sitcom or movie is a stereotype. I guarantee you NO ONE'S ever said those things in real life. This strip, however, is all of us in our OWN words. This isn't a funhouse mirror in your hands. It's an eerily accurate one. And if you're a comic geek like me, you'll have a good laugh at how well Tim's captured the voices of ALL the regulars from YOUR local shop. And then you'll hit that ONE horrible panel where you'll realize, 'Hey! I'VE said that!'"

Dan Slott, comic book writer

"It doesn't take skill to make people look bad. But it takes talent to make people look SO awful, SO grotesque, and SO vile that it's actually endearing and oddly charming. In that way, Tim reminds me of Basil Wolverton and Drew Friedman, and I can think of no higher praise."

Gail Simone, writer of *Batgirl* and *Wonder Woman*

OUR VALUED CUSTOMERS

CONVERSATIONS FROM THE COMIC BOOK STORE

TIM CHAMBERLAIN

A PERIGEE BOOK

FOR MY MOM
WHO NEVER LET US GET A NINTENDO.

A PERIGEE BOOK.
PUBLISHED BY THE PENGUIN GROUP.
PENGUIN GROUP (USA) INC.
375 HUDSON ST. NEW YORK, NEW YORK 10014. USA

PENGUIN GROUP (CANADA). 90 EGLINTON AVENUE EAST. SUITE 700. TORONTO. ONTARIO M4P 2Y3. CANADA (A DIVISION OF PEARSON PENGUIN CANADA INC.) · PENGUIN BOOKS LTD. 80 STRAND. LONDON WC2R 0RL. ENGLAND · PENGUIN GROUP IRELAND. 25 ST. STEPHEN'S GREEN. DUBLIN 2. IRELAND (A DIVISION OF PENGUIN BOOKS LTD.) · PENGUIN GROUP (AUSTRALIA). 250 CAMBERWELL ROAD. CAMBERWELL. VICTORIA 3124. AUSTRALIA (A DIVISION OF PEARSON AUSTRALIA GROUP PTY. LTD.) · PENGUIN BOOKS INDIA PVT. LTD. 11 COMMUNITY CENTRE. PANCHSHEEL PARK. NEW DELHI — 110 017. INDIA. · PENGUIN GROUP (NZ). 67 APOLLO DRIVE. ROSEDALE. AUCKLAND 0632. NEW ZEALAND. (A DIVISION OF PEARSON NEW ZEALAND LTD). PENGUIN BOOKS (SOUTH AFRICA) (PTY.) LTD. 24 STURDEE AVENUE. ROSEBANK. JOHANNESBURG 2196. SOUTH AFRICA.

PENGUIN BOOKS LTD. REGISTERED OFFICES: 80 STRAND. LONDON WC2R 0RL. ENGLAND

FIRST EDITION: JULY 2012
ISBN: 978-0-399-53752-3

PRINTED IN THE UNITED STATES OF AMERICA
10 9 8 7 6 5 4 3 2 1

AFTER I SPENT NEARLY TEN YEARS WORKING A SERIES OF LOW-PAYING RETAIL/BARISTA JOBS, I DECIDED I'D HAD ENOUGH OF CUSTOMER SERVICE AND BEGAN DOING DATA ENTRY THROUGH A TEMP SERVICE. I VOWED THAT THE ONLY WAY I WOULD EVER RETURN TO RETAIL WAS IF I COULD GET THE JOB I HAD DREAMED OF SINCE I WAS EIGHT: COMIC BOOK SHOP CLERK.

AS IT SO HAPPENS, "TEMP" STANDS FOR "TEMPORARY" AND AFTER A YEAR IN THE OFFICE, I FOUND MYSELF WORKING IN THE GLAMOROUS WORLD OF HOUSE PAINTING AND SNOW REMOVAL. SO WHEN I RECEIVED A CALL FROM MY FRIEND LULU ASKING IF I WOULD BE INTERESTED IN WORKING IN HER COMIC SHOP, I WAS OVERJOYED... BUT ALSO A BIT HESITANT.

ON THE ONE HAND, AS A LIFELONG COMIC AND SCI-FI FAN, I WAS SO EXCITED TO FINALLY BE ABLE TO HANG AROUND IN A COMIC BOOK STORE AND GET PAID. BUT AS A RECENT ESCAPEE FROM BEHIND THE CASH REGISTER, I WASN'T SURE THAT I WAS READY TO GO BACK TO RETAIL.

NEEDLESS TO SAY, I TOOK THE JOB AT THE COMIC BOOK STORE AND IT WAS EVERYTHING I HAD EVER DREAMED OF.

WHILE THERE WERE SOME LUNATICS, MOST OF THE CUSTOMERS WHO CAME INTO THE STORE WERE AWESOME. FROM OUR SUBS AND REGULARS TO THE PEOPLE WHO WERE IN THERE FOR THE FIRST TIME, THEY ALL HAD A GENUINE INTEREST AND LOVE FOR ALL THIS NERDY STUFF. THAT'S WHAT MAKES SPENDING TIME IN ANY COMIC BOOK STORE SUCH A PLEASURE. BESIDES, WHERE ELSE CAN YOU SEE ADULT MEN, FISTS CLENCHED AND RED IN THE FACE, YELLING AT EACH OTHER OVER WHICH STAR WARS BOUNTY HUNTER WOULD BEST BE ABLE TO DEFEAT BATMAN?

(TRUE STORY. AND IG-88, BY THE WAY.)

INSIDE THE PAGES OF THIS BOOK, YOU CAN SEE THE COMIC BOOK STORE THE WAY I DO — AS A PLACE THAT CELEBRATES THE HUMOROUS SIDE OF FANDOM AS WELL AS A PLACE WHERE ALL OF THAT UNCHECKED PASSION CAN GET A BIT OUT OF HAND.

THANK YOU FOR PICKING UP MY BOOK AND I HOPE YOU ENJOY **OUR VALUED CUSTOMERS** AS MUCH AS I DO.

-MR. TIM.

REGARDING HIS ENORMOUS ENERGY DRINK...

ANGRILY TO HER BOYFRIEND...
HOW IS DAREDEVIL STILL ALIVE? HOW HARD IS IT TO KILL A BLIND GUY? I'D LOVE TO WASTE THAT PRICK.
MRtiM!

TO HIS FRIEND...
I HATE SEEIN' GIRLS IN HERE. THE COMIC SHOP IS MY SANCTUARY FROM ALL THE CHICKS IN MY LIFE.
MRTIM!

WHILE DISCUSSING HIS GIRLFRIEND...
SHE'S JUST SO INCONSIDERATE. SHE KNOWS HOW IMPORTANT TRUE BLOOD IS TO ME AND SHE STILL MAKES FUN OF IT ALL THE TIME!
MRtiM!

TO HER FRIEND REGARDING THE JUSTICE LEAGUE...
I'D BE ALL "SHUT UP BATMAN! DAMN, YO. YOU AIN'T THE BOSS OF ME!"
MRtiM!

REGARDING A SHELF OF TWILIGHT BOOKS...

MRtiM!

HE WENT UP TO THE COUNTER AND ASKED...

KNOW HOW EVERYBODY WANTS TO GET WITH **HOT ANDROID LADIES?**

UH... **NO?**

OH. WELL THEY **DO.**

MRtiM!

WHILE DISCUSSING A FRIEND OF HIS...
HE READS MARVEL AND DC. YOU JUST CAN'T TRUST THAT GUY.
MRtiM!

A GOOD POINT REGARDING CATWOMAN...
IF CATWOMAN IS SO SMART AND TOGETHER THEN WHY NOT KNOCK OFF ALL THAT BURGLAR SHIT AND GET A REAL JOB?
MRTIM!

WHILE DISCUSSING THE GHOSTBUSTERS...
WHY WERE THEY AFRAID OF HIM? HE'S MADE OUT OF MARSHMALLOWS. UM... HELLO? MARSHMALLOWS AIN'T SCARY, STUPIDS.
MRHIM!

BEFORE PAYING FOR A SPIDER-MAN COMIC...

ON THE SUBJECT OF HER RECENT BREAKUP...
I JUST CAN'T BE WITH SOMEBODY WHO DOESN'T HAVE ROOM FOR EDWARD AND BELLA IN HIS LIFE.
TEAM EDWARD.
MRHIM!

OVERHEARD DURING A MAGIC TOURNAMENT...
YOU LITTLE ORC TURD! I'M NEVER LETTING YOU SHUFFLE MY DECK AGAIN!
ICP
MRHM!

WHILE CLUTCHING A PILE OF DOG-EARED PAPERS...
DO YOU WANNA BUY ANY OF THESE FROM ME? THEY'RE HARRY POTTER STORIES I FOUND ONLINE. THEY'RE REALLY SEXUAL.
NOFX
MRtiM!

TO HIS FRIEND...
SETH MACFARLANE IS THE TYLER PERRY OF ANIMATED CARTOONS.
MRtiM!

REGARDING THE KICK-ASS POSTER HANGING IN THE WINDOW...
I'M SICK OF ALL THIS MARK MILLAR MALARKEY.
MRtiM!

TO HIS WIFE...
FANTASY FOOTBALL IS JUST D&D FOR JOCKS.
MRtiM!

DURING A "WHO WOULD WIN" CONVERSATION WITH HIS FRIEND...
NO CONTEST. THE CELTICS ARE A TEAM WHILE THE X-MEN ARE A BUNCH OF LOSERS, ALL OUT FOR THEMSELVES.
MRTIM!

TO HER FRIEND WHILE DISCUSSING ADULT RELATIONSHIPS...
THAT BUFFY CHICK? YEAH, I'D HOOK UP WITH HER... BUT ONLY TO PISS OFF MY HUSBAND.
MRtiM!

REGARDING THE COVER OF A RECENT CATWOMAN COMIC...

HE CAME UP TO THE COUNTER AND ASKED...

WHILE TRYING TO RETURN A PACK OF POKÊMON CARDS...

TO HIS GIRLFRIEND...
I WISH THERE WERE COMIC BOOK POLICE AND I COULD CALL'EM AND BE LIKE "HEY! THEY'RE FUCKIN' UP BATMAN WITH A DUMB STORY! GET'EM!!"
MRtiM!

REGARDING BATGIRL'S LACK OF PHYSICAL IMPAIRMENT...
NOT TO BE DRAMATIC BUT SEEING BARBARA GORDON WALK MAKES ME WANNA KILL MYSELF.
MRTIM!

REGARDING MAC's LINE OF WONDER WOMAN THEMED MAKEUP...
IT'S THE SAME EXACT MAKEUP THAT WONDER WOMAN USES.
MRtiM!

TO HIS FRIEND...
IN REAL LIFE BRUCE CAMPBELL DOESN'T ACT LIKE ASH AT ALL. MY COUSIN SAYS HE'S JUST SOME REGULAR GUY. DOESN'T THAT SUCK?
THE WALKING
MRtiM!

TO HER FRIEND REGARDING THE RECENT ENERGY CRISIS...
WE SHOULD ALL JUST GO BACK TO USING STEAMPUNK TECHNOLOGY TO RUN EVERY-THING. LIKE BACK IN THE 1960s OR WHATEVER.
MRtiM!
CBGB

TO HIS FRIEND WHILE UNAWARE OF THE POSTAGE STAMP SIZED DORITO CHIP ON HIS FACE....
EVERYONE AT MY JOB IS SO FUCKIN' STUPID. I'M THE SMARTEST ONE THERE AN' I'M ALWAYS TELLING THEM THEY'RE DOING STUFF WRONG BUT THEY'RE SO STUPID.
adidas
MRtiM!

TO ANOTHER MOM IN THE STORE...
MY SON SKYLAR, HE'S ONLY 5 BUT HE ALREADY FEELS THAT COMICS ARE CHILDISH. HE PREFERS GRAPHIC NOVELS.
MRtiM!

AFTER I COMPLIMENTED HIS SUPERBOY T-SHIRT...

YO. IT'S SUPERMAN. IT AIN'T SUPERBOY. I AIN'T NO BOY MAH' FUCKA.

MRTIM!

TO HIS MOTHER AS SHE TRIED TO LEAVE THE STORE WITHOUT BUYING A PACK OF YU-GI-OH CARDS...
YOU CAN'T LEAVE, YOU DIDN'T BUY ME ANYTHING! I WANT THIS AND YOU HAVE TO GET ME IT! DON'T BE A BUTTWIPE!!
YOU LOOKED BETTER ONLINE
MRtiM!

REGARDING A THOR POSTER...
THAT MOVIE'S GONNA SUCK AND THOR'S LAME ANYWAYS. HE'S NOT A SUPERHERO. HE'S JUST AN OLD BIBLE CHARACTER.
MRtiM!

TO HIS FRIEND...
SO HE SAW MY SHIRT AN' SAID "HEY BATMAN!" AN I WAS LIKE "I'M NOT REALLY BATMAN, DAD." MY DAD'S SUCH A FUCKING IDIOT!
MRtiM!

A MOMENT OF CLARITY AS HE PAID FOR HIS COMICS...
SOMETIMES I FEEL LIKE IT WILL **NEVER** BE ENOUGH AND I'LL **NEVER** HAVE ENOUGH **COMICS.**
MRtiM!

I WISH I HAD HEARD THE BEGINNING OF THIS CONVERSATION...
YEAH WELL I'M PRETTY SURE THEY WOULDN'T LET YOU BRING ANY GODDAMN **MOUNTAIN DEW** IN THE FUCKIN' **DANGER ROOM** SO JUST **DROP IT!**
MRTIM!

TO HIS FRIEND WHILE THEY LOOKED THROUGH BACK ISSUES...
OH MAN. WOULDN'T IT SUCK IF THOUGHT BUBBLES WERE REAL? THEN PEOPLE WOULD KNOW ALL THE GROSS STUFF THAT I THINK ABOUT.
MRTIM!

TO HER FRIEND WHILE THEY DISCUSSED SUPERHEROES...
IT MUST BE SO GROSS TO KISS COLOSSUS. I BET HE TASTES LIKE PENNIES.
FRAGGLE ROCK
MRTIM!

WHILE DISCUSSING BATMAN...
IT'D BE AWESOME IF BATMAN'S PARENTS DIDN'T DIE, THEY JUST GOT DIVORCED AND HE MADE UP THEM GETTIN' KILLED CUZ HE'S JUST A BIG BABY.
4
MRTIM!

WHILE DISCUSSING GIRLS...

WHILE LOOKING THROUGH THE NEW ARRIVALS RACK...
I BET IT'S SO SCARY TO FIGHT WONDER WOMAN. ESPECIALLY WHEN SHE'S ON HER PERIOD. SHE MUST GET FUCKING CRAZY.
MRtiM!

AFTER HIS FRIEND RECOMMENDED THAT HE WATCH DOCTOR WHO...
SOME GEEK FLIES AROUND TIME IN A PHONE BOOTH? THAT'S JUST A DUMBASS **BILL AND TED RIP OFF.**
4
MRTIM!

TO HIS FRIEND...
I SAW HOW SHE SMILED WHEN THOR TOOK HIS SHIRT OFF...I HATE HOW DISRESPECTFUL SHE IS TO ME.
MRtiM!

TO HIS FRIEND WHILE DISCUSSING WHAT THEY WOULD CHANGE ABOUT COMICS...
WHEN I START WORKIN' AT DC I'M GONNA MAKE IT SO THEY CAN SHOW TITS IN THEIR COMICS.
MRtiM!

TO HIS MOTHER...
BUT MA... I NEED IT! IF YOU GET ME IT THEN PEOPLE WILL BE AFRAID OF ME!
MRtiM!

WHILE TRYING TO IMRESS A FEMALE CUSTOMER...
YOU GOTTA UNDERSTAND WOLVERINE TO READ HIS COMICS. SEE I'VE SEEN THE SAME HARD TIMES AS HIM SO I REALLY **GET** HIM.
SUBLIME
MRtiM!

REGARDING GOTHAM CITY'S FLAWED CRIMINAL REHABILITATION SYSTEM...
WHY DO THEY STILL BOTHER LOCKING UP BAD GUYS IN ARKHAM? THEY ALL JUST BREAK OUT OF THERE ANYWAY, WHAT'S THE POINT?
MRTIM!

WHILE DISCUSSING THE LOVE LIFE OF SUPERVILLAINS . . .

SOMETIMES I THINK THE JOKER WILL **NEVER** STEP UP AND DO RIGHT BY **HARLEY.**

MRtiM!

TO HIS FRIEND...
SOMETIMES I THINK THAT BITCH IS JUST PRETENDING TO BE INTO COMICS SO SHE CAN GET WITH ME.
MRtiM!

A REALIZATION WHILE WAITING IN LINE...
DO YOU EVER FEEL LIKE MARVEL IS FUCKING WITH US?
4
MRtiM!

WHILE WAITING IN LINE...
SOMETIMES I GET SO WORKED UP WHEN I'M READIN' MY COMICS THAT I HAVE TO DRINK LIKE 5 OR 6 BEERS AFTER.
MRtiM!

ANGRILY TO HIS FRIEND...
I COULD TELL THAT SHE LIKED X-MEN JUST BY LOOKIN' AT HER. SHE HAS THAT KIND OF FACE.
MRtiM!

REGARDING A PHOTO OF PRINCESS LEIA HUGGING CHEWBACCA...
OH MAN! THAT GORILLA IS GOING TO RAPE THAT GIRL!
MRtiM!

TO HIS FRIEND WHILE THEY LOOKED AT BATMAN COMICS...
THIS SHIT IS LAME. LOOK. BATGIRL? WHAT NEXT? SUPERMAN-GIRL OR SOME SHIT? COMIC BOOKS ARE SO DUMB.
TAPOUT
MRHIM!

REGARDING HIS G.I. JOE AND LEGEND OF ZELDA TATTOOS...
MY TATTOOS ARE ALL FROM ALTERNATIVE CULTURE SO MOST PEOPLE DON'T KNOW WHAT THEY ARE.
MRtiM!

THE SECRET TO A SUCCESSSFUL CAREER IN COMICS REVEALED!
ALL YOU HAVE TO DO IS MAKE A COMIC THAT THEY WANNA MAKE A MOVIE OUT OF.
MRTIM!

TO HIS FRIEND REGARDING RETURN OF THE JEDI . . .

MY FAVORITE PART IS WHEN ALL A THEM EWOKS GET **KILLED.**

MRtiM!

ON THE SUBJECT OF SPIDER-MAN...
VENOM AND GREEN GOBLIN AND ALL OF THOSE GUYS ARE DICKS. IT'S SO UNFAIR HOW THEY ALL JUST KEEP GOING AFTER SPIDER-MAN.
MRtiM!

TO HIS TEENAGE BROTHER...
YOU GOTTA BE DONE WITH COMICS WHEN YOU'RE IN COLLEGE. CHICKS DON'T WANNA BANG SOME GEEK.
BUD LIGHT
MRTIM!

WHILE DISCUSSING SUPERVILLAINS...
IF I WAS MAGNETO I'D SPEND ALL DAY MESSIN' WITH PROFESSOR X AN' HIS STUPID ASS METAL WHEELCHAIR.
MRTIM!

REGARDING A WOLVERINE T-SHIRT...

WHILE WAITING IN LINE...
SPIDER-MAN IS A WIMP. HE'D NEVER MAKE IT IN NEW YORK.
SCOTT PILGRIM
MRTIM!

TO ANOTHER MOM IN THE STORE...
MY SON TREVIN ONLY READS BOOKS THAT ARE BASED ON MOVIES. THAT WAY HE ALREADY KNOWS HOW THEY END AND HE WON'T GET TOO ANXIOUS.
MRTIM!

REGARDING THE CAPTAIN AMERICA SHIELD HANGING IN THE STORE...
OH MAN! OH MAN, LOOKIT! IT'S THE ONE! THE SHIELD! THE CAPTAIN SHIELD! THE ONE HE HAS! THE REAL ONE! OH MAN! WOW! OH MY GOD!
MRtIM!

AS HIS MOM DRAGGED HIM OUT OF THE STORE...

TO HIS FRIEND AS THEY WALKED INTO THE STORE...
THEN HE SAYS HE WON'T PAY MY RENT JUST CUZ THE LAST TIME I SPENT IT ON WEED AN' COMICS AN' I'M ALL LIKE "QUIT HATIN' DAD!"
MRtiM!

WHILE HER ADULT SON LOOKED THROUGH THE NEW ARRIVALS RACK...
MY SON MAKES ME TAKE HIM TO STORES LIKE THIS ALL THE TIME. YOU BOYS ALL NEED TO FUCKING GROW UP.
#1 GRANDMA
MRTIM!

TO HIS GIRLFRIEND AFTER SHE JOKED THAT HE HAD TOO MUCH GREEN LANTERN STUFF...
YEAH? WELL WHO SAYS SUPERMAN'S SO GREAT? JUST CUZ HE CAN FLY AND HE'S ALL STRONG AN' HANDSOME AN' SHIT? SO WHAT.
MRHIM!

REGARDING A SUPERGIRL POSTER HANGING IN THE STORE...

MAN. LOOKIT THE TITS ON THAT ONE. IF I WERE WORKIN' UP IN HERE, I'D JUST **STARE** AT 'EM ALL DAY LONG. THIS JOB MUST **RULE.**

MRTIM!

EXCITEDLY TO HIS FRIEND...
OH DUDE. IF I WAS WOLVERINE? I'D BE ALL LIKE DUDE. OOH I'D BE LIKE, OH MAN I WOULD BE SO LIKE, DUDE. SERIOUSLY, YOU DON'T EVEN WANNA KNOW.
MRTIM!

TO HER FRIEND WHILE DISCUSSING WHAT HER ENGLISH TEACHER HAD TOLD HER...
HE SAID OF ALL THE SUPERHERO FAN FICTION HE'S READ THIS YEAR, MINE IS **BY FAR** THE MOST **EROTIC.** ISN'T THAT GREAT?
MRTIM!

TO HER FRIEND...
SO MY IDIOT MOTHER SENT ME POKÉMON CARDS WHEN I TOLD HER TO BUY ME YU-GI-OH CARDS. I SWEAR... SHE IS SÖ USELESS.
I ♥ Hogwarts
MRTIM!

REGARDING A TRON: LEGACY POSTER...
WHY'D THEY PUT A GIRL IN THE MOVIE? SHE'S JUST GONNA DISTRACT ME FROM THE STORY!
MRtiM!

WHILE WAITING IN LINE...
IF I EVER GET MARRIED AND MY WIFE DOESN'T WANT A STAR WARS WEDDING, I'M GONNA DUMP THAT CHICK ON THE SPOT.
MRtiM!

TO HER FRIEND WHILE DISCUSSING HER CURRENT RELATIONSHIP...

TO HIS FRIEND...
I SAW "X-FACTOR" ON THE CABLE MENU AND I GOT SO EXCITED BUT THEN I SAW WHAT X-FACTOR REALLY WAS AND I WAS THE OPPOSITE OF EXCITED.
MRtiM!

TO HIS FRIEND WHILE THEY DISCUSSED X-MEN COMICS...

SHE ASKED...
MY BOYFRIEND IS INTO LIKE, MURDER AND DEATH. DO YOU HAVE A SECTION FOR THAT?
ROCK STAR!
MRtiM!

WHILE DISCUSSING THE ATTRACTIVENESS OF SUPERHEROES...
I DON'T LIKE SUPERGIRL. SHE'S GOT WEIRD KNEES.
MRtiM!

TO A FEMALE CUSTOMER...
SEE WHAT I MEAN? I TOLD YOU, I REALLY LIKE BATMAN.
MRtiM!

TO HIS FRIEND...
DO I LOOK LIKE I'M MADE OF SNACKWRAPS BITCH?
MRtiM!

TO HIS FRIEND...
I WISH THAT GIRLS WERE AS COOL AS DRAGONS.
MRtiM!

WHILE CRITICIZING THE ARTWORK IN A SUPERMAN COMIC...
YEAH. THIS GUY NEEDS TO LIKE, GO BACK TO LIKE...COMIC DRAWRING SCHOOL, OR LIKE, COMIC BOOK LIKE, COMIC DRAWER COLLEGE OR WHATEVER. HE SHOULD GO BACK THERE.
MRtIM!

HE RUSHED INTO THE STORE AND FRANTICALLY ASKED...
YOU GOT BATMOBILE?
MRtiM!

TO HER FRIEND WHILE THEY SHOPPED FOR A PRESENT FOR HER SON...
I MEAN, HE'S TURNING 8. THAT LITTLE CREEP'S TOO OLD FOR THAT SPIDER-MAN CRAP ANYWAYS.
ZOO·YORK
MRtiM!

WHILE PAYING FOR HIS COMICS...
WELL, IF SPIDER-MAN IS SO GREAT THEN WHY IS EVERYBODY ALWAYS TRYING TO KILL HIM?
MRTIM!

TO HIS ELDERLY MOTHER ON THEIR WAY INTO THE STORE...
I DON'T FUCKING CARE MOM. I WASN'T GONNA RUN FOR THE BUS. THESE ARE MY GOOD SWEAT PANTS!
MRtiM!

REGARDING A PLASTIC THOR HAMMER REPLICA...

WISH I COULD GET MY HANDS ON THE **REAL THOR HAMMER.** I'D TAKE IT TO WORK AND LAY WASTE TO **EVERYONE** IN THE WHOLE **HOSPITAL.**

MRHIM!

WHILE TALKING DOWN TO HER MOTHER...
ALL MY FAVORITE MOVIES ARE INDEPENDENT '80s MOVIES LIKE THE BREAKFAST CLUB AND STUFF SO YOU PROBABLY DON'T KNOW ANY OF THEM.
devil wears prada
MRtiM!

TO HIS GIRLFRIEND...
I BET I COULD BEAT THE FLASH IF I HAD A CAR. SERIOUSLY. HE PROBABLY AIN'T FASTER THAN A CAR.
MRtiM!

MR. TIM LIVES IN A LARGE AMERICAN CITY WITH A GIRL AND SOME CATS. HE SPENDS HIS TIME DRAWING, DRINKING BEER WITH HIS BROTHERS AND DIGGING THROUGH QUARTER COMIC BINS ON WEEKENDS WITH THE GANG.

THANKS → SANNY · MA · POPS · THERMOS · DAN'T HANK · LULU · DAN WARS · HATRACK · LILLY · MEG LEDER